W9-DEU-853

THE LITTLE BOOK OF

OFFICE SPELLS

Other Books by Sophia

The Little Book of Love Spells
The Little Book of Hexes for Women

Sophia's Web site:
www.psychicsophia.com

The Little Book of
Office Spells

Sophia

**Andrews McMeel
Publishing**

Kansas City

THIS BOOK IS DEDICATED TO CARL B. ERICKSON,
A BELIEVER IN DEMOCRATIC PRINCIPLES

www.andrewsmcmeel.com

99 00 01 02 03 RDC 10 9 8 7 6 5 4 3 2 1

Library of Congress Catalog Card Number: 98-48179
ISBN: 0-8362-8182-9

Composed by Kelly & Company, Lee's Summit, MO
another idea from becker&mayer!

ATTENTION: SCHOOLS AND BUSINESSES
Andrews McMeel books are available at quantity discounts with bulk purchase for educational, business, or sales promotional use. For information, please write to:
Special Sales Department, Andrews McMeel Publishing, 4520 Main Street, Kansas City, Missouri 64111.

Introduction

Wouldn't it just be great if someday you could walk into your office or workplace, wave your magic wand, and—*poof!*—everything would be just the way you wanted it to be? Of course, in that case, you would suddenly be on a beach in Tahiti with a huge lottery check in the bank, right? Work is not something we do for fun. It is the worm in the apple of life. Yet the difference between a pleasant work environment and an awful one can simply add or take years from your life. And your HMO doesn't cover work-related mental breakdowns, I'll bet. Well, the worst thing about working (aside from, well, working itself) is the powerlessness one feels. Whether you are downsized, overloaded, harassed, ignored, or generally put upon, you know that being a worker of the world nowadays is rough, right? But never fear! That complaint box or *(shudder)* quality-control meeting may not do zip to help you, but this little book will!

Harassed? Light a candle! Want a raise? Chant a bit. Need to get rid of a nasty coworker? Burn a few herbs. Will these spells work? Well, there is only one way to find out. . . .

The power of magic lies deep within us. Our subconscious is waiting to be tapped to unleash the power of our Wills. Sometimes we need assistance with that and a little psychic (or psychological) boost may help take us where we want to go. A little success goes a long way if you are following your True Will.

With this little book you can bring others into line and, maybe, mysteriously fly to the top of the corporate ladder. Wonder how others have made it and if they had a little spooky help? Well, they just might have. These spells are said to be tried and true; some have been passed down in my family for generations. They are never a guarantee for life to happen the way you want it to, but they can't hurt, and maybe they will actually help make a situation a win-win one!

Of course this is simply a gag book, a jolly, stress-relieving book to read aloud at happy hour in your favorite watering hole or over a raucous venting lunch! Or . . . is it something else? You decide: At work, who will get the last laugh?

I've tried to cover every possible situation, but I know I've left out a few (Spamming on the Internet!). You should feel free to improvise and alter the spells you see any way you want. Be creative, have fun at work! But remember, there is no spell better than using your head, standing up to bullies and jerks, having a great sense of humor, and realizing your own real value. There is no magic to replace these essential traits of the modern Surviving Worker.

A final note: The prime law of office spells (and life) is that what goes around comes around, and that one should always work and play well with others.

So off to work you go with your lunch box and your new handy little book. If you use it wisely, maybe the job will mellow out, you can all have fun, and maybe, if there's time, get a bit of actual work accomplished.

Work hard! Play hard! Spell hard!

—Sophia

P.S. And always have fun!

Cinch That Interview Spell

Okay, now you have a foot in the door, but that's about all! An office visit and a nice chat are not enough. You have to land this job by turning on the charm and getting them to want you! This spell will get them excited about you and in no time you'll be glowing in that new position—just make sure you want it!

You Will Need
+ an oak leaf
+ a bit of sugared ginger

The Spell
Before the interview, straighten your nice clothes and then place pieces of the oak leaf in each shoe. Step into the shoes and, as you do so, say:

> MIGHTY OAK AM I
> ROOTS DOWN INTO EARTH
> BRANCHES FILL THE SKY
> BRING MY DREAM TO BIRTH!

Jump once and feel the force of your wish echo out!
Then, chew a bit of sugared ginger and say:

> MY WORDS BE SWEET
> TO ALL I MEET
> MY OPINION BE DEAR
> TO ALL WHO HEAR!

Go to the interview and before you enter, say:

> BY TREE OF SUN
> AND HERB OF FIRE
> I SHALL NOW GAIN
> WHAT I DESIRE!

Go knock 'em dead!

The Successful Presentation Spell

Nothing is more terrifying than standing up in front of a group of people and presenting something. We all know that the number of things that can go wrong is infinite—and that doesn't even include the quality of the material! This little spell will give you self-confidence and keep the bad (or weird) luck at bay until your time is done. Want 'em applauding? First put together a crackerjack presentation and then try this!

You Will Need
+ a feather
+ one lavender flower
+ some light blue thread

THE SPELL
At noon on a beautiful day, go someplace calm and
quiet, and pull out the items. First, hold the feather
up to the sun and say:

> FEATHER OF TRUTH
> FEATHER OF LIGHT
> MAKE MY WORDS GLOW
> FILL THEM WITH MIGHT!
> MAT!

Then take the lavender flower and
touch it to the ground, saying:

> HERB OF EARTH AND AIR COMBINED
> BIND SUCCESS TO MY WORDS
> MAKE THEM ENTWINED
> AS A HAWK WINGING OUT
> MAY THIS SPELL UNWIND!
> HERU!

Bind the two together with the thread, holding them to your heart, and feel all the energies come together. Then say:

SUN AND AIR
EARTH AND FLOWER
THREAD AND FEATHER
MY WORDS ARE POWER!
MA RA HA!

Put this away and keep it safe. When needed, put it in a pocket just before your presentation. They will hang on your every word!

The Business Hunch Spell

This is more a divination or a spell for discovering the will of the gods than an outright act of magic. As a form of *bibliomancy*, or using a book as an omen-getting device, it's very simple but works well. If you have an important business decision to make regarding a certain matter, this spell will instantly give you clear advice. Just let your fingers do the walking!

You Will Need
+ a gray candle
+ matches
+ a small piece of paper
+ a book*

* The book must be related to the question. For example, if you are making a decision about an oil company, you can use their prospectus or a book about oil. I recently had a question about my computer and I used the Macintosh instruction manual.

THE SPELL
Around dusk, or even better under a waxing moon,
light the candle and say:

As a flame
I focus here
That an answer
May be clear

Write your question on the paper, making it as concise as
possible. Place this under the candle while repeating the
question three times. Then, pick up the book and say:

Winds of Hermes
Words of Hermes
Thoughts of Hermes
Money of Hermes
Center here
Make all clear!

Close your eyes, spin the book about in your hands every which way, and repeat your question one more time. Open the book at random and point! The word you get will answer your question. If you hit a blank space, then this is not the right time to ask the question. When you're finished, write the word on the paper and burn it. Let the ashes float out a window and thank Hermes for the help!

SPELL FOR A STRESS-FREE OFFICE PARTY

Okay, it's office party time! Do I hear a groan? a gripe?
Worried about the furnishings and reputations getting
scarred? strange spills? stranger day-after tales? Do this
little spell in the early morning before the party and
things will be so calm and fun and warm that you'll
have nothing to gossip about in the coming weeks!
Wait a minute . . . is this a good thing? Anyway,
keep the peace and start the festivities right!

You Will Need
+ some small green pine branches
+ a green candle
+ matches

The Spell
On a Thursday at noon, say:

GREEN OF LIFE
GREEN OF PEACE
OUT GOES STRIFE
STRESS RELEASE!

Scatter or place the pine branches around the room, saying:

IN FLOWS CALM
HATE FLOWS AWAY
ALL IS WELL
AND SO IT SHALL STAY

In the center of the branches, light the green candle, and say:

AS THE SHINING SUN GROWS BRIGHT
I CALL IN THE HEALING LIGHT
PEACE BY DAY
PEACE BY NIGHT
MAY PEACE IN EVERY HEART IGNITE!
PAX AMOR!

Excellent Contract Spell

This is a *big* one and you can't afford to let it get away.
Contracts are slippery; push too hard or don't try hard
enough and they slip right through your fingers. This little
spell will help you hook and land that big contract, and
won't everyone be pleased with you!

You Will Need
+ a copy of the contract
+ some stationery or a letter from
the person you wish to sign it
+ a small, gray, squarish stone
+ a piece of blue ribbon

The Spell
Late at night, on a Saturday, take the contract and hold it to
the four directions and then the center, saying each time:

Janus bind
Janus bless
Bound this will be
Grant it success!

Place the client's paper face down on top of the contract,
roll them up, and touch the floor with them, saying:

Janus together
Our rivers will flow
A tree setting roots
Together we'll grow

Bind the rolled-up papers as shown. Place the stone on top
covered by the ribbon. Wrap it clockwise about the papers so
that the stone is held fast, saying:

Janus bind
And bind again
Until I will it
This binding won't end!

Keep this deep in your desk, locked away. When you land the contract, bury it near water and pat yourself on the back.

Magnetic Résumé Spell

This spell will attract much attention to your little résumé as it competes with hundreds of others! Putting that extra little zing on your résumé will really help you get that callback, and who knows where that will lead?

You Will Need
+ some fern tops that you picked on the full moon
(any ferns will do)
+ matches
+ a pile of your résumés
+ a small magnet

The Spell
Dry the fern tops, and at night during the next full moon, place the small pile of dried fern in a dish. Light the fern on

fire and let it smolder. Pass the résumés through
the smoke seven times, saying:

> BONA FORTUNA
> COME TO ME
> I SEND OUT MY WILL
> SO MAY IT BE
> BRING ME ATTENTION
> AND PROSPERITY!
> BONA FORTUNA
> COME TO ME!

Then take one of the résumés and roll the small magnet
up in it, twisting both ends. Hold it tight and fill it
with your energy, saying:

> I CONJURE THEE, MAGNET,
> BRING NOW TO ME
> ALL JOBS I DESIRE

SO MAY IT BE!
BONA FORTUNA
COME SET ME FREE!

Send out the résumés and keep the "magnetized" one in your desk drawer or some such place. Soon people will be drawn to your résumé. The rest is up to you!

CHECKING THE STOCKS SPELL

Everyone knows that smart investors dump their stocks before they dive—buy low and sell high, right? But how do the really gifted brokers and regular folk *know* when a stock will do well or needs to be tossed? Many are psychic, whether they know it or not, and some may use a spell like this one—if they don't, they should! So get an edge on the competition and let the powers help you out!

You Will Need

+ a silver ring (or earring) that you have worn
+ a piece of green thread
+ a newspaper with the stock quotes
+ a green highlighter pen

THE SPELL

First, at midnight on a Thursday, tie one end of the thread on the ring so it makes a pendulum. Hold the ring between your hands for one minute and say over and over:

DISC OF EARTH
CIRCLE OF MIND
TELL ME TRUTH
WHETHER CRUEL OR KIND
BY THE POWER WITHIN ME
AS I WILL SO MAY IT BE!

When ready to use it, open the paper to the stock section and use the green highlighter to mark the stocks you are interested in. Don't choose more than ten for each session. Hang the pendulum over the first stock quote, holding the thread by thumb and forefinger, and say:

UP, DOWN
IN OR OUT
SHOW THE TRUTH
AROUND AND ABOUT!

If the pendulum swings back and forth, it means
the stock will go down.

If it swings from left to right it will go down a little.

If it swings toward and away from you it will go down a lot.

If the pendulum turns in circles the stock will go up;
if it rotates clockwise it will rise a lot, and if
counterclockwise, just a little.

Repeat this chant and process for each stock quote.

Get the Right Employee Spell

In front of you is a pile of résumés (or letters), each representing a possible future employee. Logically, you have eliminated the lemons and these are all apples. But which ones will fit in and not be full of worms? Hard to tell these days—unless of course you use this little beauty of a spell to weed out the rotten ones!

You Will Need
+ a pinch of salt
+ a new deck of playing cards
that has never been used
+ a small purple candle
+ matches

THE SPELL

At twilight, on a Tuesday, lay all the "finalist" résumés out on a table or, if necessary, the floor. Scatter the pinch of salt over them, saying:

> BEGONE ALL BLOCKS
> BEGONE EVERY LIE
> BEGONE ALL BAD WORKERS
> GOOD WORKERS TO ME FLY
> BONUM ARTIFEX!

After opening the new deck of cards, light the candle and pass the cards over the candle eight times, saying:

> HEARTS OF FEELING
> SPADES OF STRENGTH
> DIAMONDS OF MONEY
> CLUBS OF WORK
> REVEAL TO ME
> THE TRUTHS THAT LURK
> BONUM ARTIFEX!

Concentrate on specifically who you want for the position(s) you are seeking to fill, in terms of their qualities, their strengths, and so forth, while you shuffle the cards really well. Then place three cards up on each résumé.

You want to pursue people who have drawn high-numbered hearts, diamonds, and clubs—low spades are also acceptable, but not high ones. What you are really looking for are the aces, as these are the most intense. If potential employees draw an ace of hearts, they'll be lovely and loving; ace of diamonds, they'll make much money for the company; ace of clubs, they'll be hard workers; ace of spades: trouble!

Hire the good aces!

Hex Against Lameness

"Oh! I was just about to call you back. . . ." "I couldn't do it, sorry! I was at a meeting!" "It is here on my desk somewhere, let me get back to you." "Are you sure I said that? Well, it's not on my calendar. . . ." We have all heard the same sorts of wimpy, whiny, ridiculous stories, and we all think the same thing: *What a lame excuse!* What is a person to do? It seems that incompetence breeds. It goes from one idiot to another—lameness is a social disease! Well here is a hex to banish lameness from your office and from your business life. When faced with the wrath-inducing terminal lameness of someone, send a psychic wake-up call!

YOU WILL NEED
+ a piece of red thread
+ a blue votive candle
+ matches
+ a paper clip

THE SPELL
Optional: Write the initials of the lame offender with
the paper clip on the candle before you begin.

Tie the thread around the candle and light the candle.
Repeat the following words:

CANDLE BLUE AND BURNING BRIGHT
RID US OF LAMENESS AND STRIFE
PUT THE RUDE LAME ONES TO FLIGHT
MAY I HAVE A LAMELESS LIFE!
SVAHA!

Now, stare into the flame as you unfold
the paper clip and say:

UNFOLD AND THEN RELEASE
LAMENESS DECREASE
YOUR SLACKNESS WILL NOT GAIN
NO LAMENESS WILL REMAIN
SVAHA!

Pierce the candle with the paper clip and extinguish the
flame. Toss the whole thing into a Dumpster, imagining all
the lame excuses going with it. *Sigh*, what a relief!

The R-E-S-P-E-C-T Spell

"Sock it to me, sock it to me, sock it to me . . . RESPECT!"
Don't we all deserve it? You bet your First Amendment
we do! You're not asking for too much at work, right?
Just a little respect. It is not that others need to bow down
and worship you, although that would be nice. It's more
that you actually have a brain (unlike some of your
coworkers). You have earned the right to have others
treat you with respect and honor—or else! Here is the
"or else": This is a spell to raise some eyebrows and
a few thumbs up. Rrrrr! Go get some R-E-S-P-E-C-T!

You Will Need
+ some rose oil and musk oil
+ a small glass or crystal cup

THE SPELL

At noon on a Sunday, pour the rose oil into the crystal cup and put it in the sunlight as you say:

> I AM FIRE AND LIGHT
> WORTHY OF TRUST
> SHINING AND BRIGHT
> RESPECT ME YOU MUST!
> LUX FIAT!

At midnight, expose the cup to the night air and, if possible, moonlight. Add the musk oil and say:

> I AM ICE AND NIGHT
> POWERFUL AND STILL
> BRINGER OF FRIGHT
> RESPECT ME YOU WILL!
> NOX FIAT!

Mix the oils together with the thumb on your left hand
and rub it on your neck, heart, and belly, then say:

> LUX FIAT NOX FIAT
> I AM DARKNESS AND LIGHT
> ALL WILL RESPECT ME
> AND FEEL MY MIGHT!

Do this before work each day for one full week and by
the end of the week they'll be respecting your bumpkiss!

PSYCHO TEMP FROM HELL HEX

How can one person cause so many problems in such a short time? Not only did he download your hard drive into the trash, he alienated all your best customers, lost more than a few messages, and the telephone system will probably never work right again. All this mayhem and havoc was caused in an amazingly short time, like a tornado. And it is Psycho Temp from Hell who just caused it all. Do this bad-temp-worker spell before your blood pressure soars and someone calls the police because the temp has been trashed. This little hex may well get your life back into perspective. This spell also works on horrid domestic help, terrible laborers, and people from (shudder) other departments who are sent to you to "help out."

You Will Need
+ a leaf of a willow tree
+ a piece of paper the temp has touched or written on

The Spell
Take the willow leaf and walk around the temp's area of destruction counterclockwise three times and say:

Take this one away
Take this one away
Do it tomorrow
If not today!
Expellatus!

Put the leaf into the paper and make a paper airplane out of it with the leaf inside. Open a window or go outside and say:

Of damage you're the cause
Your bad work gives pause
By cosmic rules and laws
Begone!

Toss the paper airplane out the window and see that bad
temp fly out with it—speak out the window:

EXPELLATUS EST!

And slam it shut. Good riddance to bad rubbish!

The Child Care Protection Spell

Nobody wants to leave her child in a less than desirable day-care facility. And let's face it, there is no day care good enough for your little jewel, right? The sad fact is that you do have to work and so you leave your precious child and wonder if they're all right or . . . we all have imaginations. No spell works better than intuition! Does the day care "feel" right? If not, pull your child out! Common sense is the best judge. But, to hedge your bets, here is a spell my grandmother taught me that will help you and your wee one feel safe.

You Will Need
+ a lucky penny that you both found on the sidewalk
+ a piece of cedar bark
+ a small "Apache tear" stone
+ a white handkerchief
+ a piece of white string
+ a felt pen (your child's favorite color)

THE SPELL

At sunset, collect these things with your child. Together, put the penny, cedar bark, and the Apache tear stone in the handkerchief, gather it up, and tie a piece of white string around it to give the "doll" a head. Then say, with your child:

THE TIES THAT BIND
THE UMBILICAL CORD
FROM ME TO YOU
WILL NOT COME UNDONE
THAT MUCH IS TRUE.
MAY THE HEAVENS WATCH OVER YOU
UNTIL MY RETURN.
MAY YOU HAVE JOY
AND EVERY DAY LEARN!
HABONDIA TUERI!

Next, kiss your child on the head. Draw a happy face on the
doll and place it in your child's pocket or backpack. My
grandmother used to tell me to check my pockets for my
lucky doll if I felt insecure. It worked better then carrying
around a picture and you can always send that babe a shot
of love through the doll at any time during the day.

No Mercy Anti-Sexual Harassment Hex

It may or may not have happened in the actual Oval Office, but just the same, it happened to you or a coworker. There you were, minding your own business, when suddenly— the sexual shark attack. You got the "offer of a lifetime," or at least that is how the sleazebag sees it. You, on the other hand, see it as harassment.

Or maybe the actual attack has yet to happen; the hormone-filled creep is circling like a buzzard and working up to outright harassment. Hose him down before he gets too revved up! This little spell will do the trick. Of course, document, document, document then—if the spell doesn't stop it, sue the child-of-unmarried-parents!

YOU WILL NEED
+ a black candle
+ matches
+ a steel needle
+ a paper the harasser has touched or ideally signed
+ a white feather

THE SPELL
At midnight on a Saturday, light the candle and pierce
the paper with a needle, saying:

YOU STUCK IT TO ME
I NOW STICK THEE
BY WORD AND SPELL
GO TO HELL!

Burn the paper, all the time concentrating on making the harasser feel all you feel, all the pain and humiliation. Keep focused on your intent while picking up the white feather and waving it over the candle as you say:

ÍPSOS!

Put out the candle with the feather. The next day, secretly drop the needle on the desk of the harasser. The unwanted attention should stop. If it happens again, repeat—then sue!

Pay Raise Power Spell

Overworked and underpaid: the mantra of the decade!
Prices keep going up, it seems, faster than wages! How to
pay for all the little necessities of life? Can't live without
a few luxuries too, right? The answer is simple: You need
a raise! Try burning the candle (this one!) at both ends
and watch that paycheck pump a little more weight!

You Will Need
+ a green candle
+ a second smaller candle (yellow)
+ matches
+ catnip
+ a pay stub

THE SPELL

On the day of the new moon, assemble everything in the morning before leaving for work. Light the small yellow candle, hold the catnip and pay stub in both hands, and say:

> HERB OF MONEY
> TOKEN OF PAY
> ATTRACT MORE CASH
> BEGIN SO TODAY!
> AVE DIVITAE!

From the small candle, drip some wax onto the green candle's side, press the catnip and stub into the wax, and drip more wax on it until they are sealed onto the candle. Place the green candle into a holder; place the holder on a dish.

Light the green candle with the small candle, blow out the small candle, and say:

AVE DIVITAE!
BRING NOW TO ME
AN INCREASE IN WEALTH
FOR ALL TO SEE
AVE DIVITAE!
SO MAKE IT BE!

Burn the green candle for a short time, blow it out, and go to work.

Light the green candle and repeat the above verse every morning until the full moon. That night, do it one last time, but repeat the verse three times. Let the candle burn completely down (keep an eye on it!) and then go to bed happy.

Fortune will smile on you soon and you can treat yourself to that new toy you've been eyeing!

Sweetening Up the Supervisor

It's never perfect, it seems, being an employee. There is always someone above you and *that* means that you have to care about her opinion! It's all so complicated, even if the boss is basically okay. This little bolt from the blue will sweeten your boss's attitude toward you and help things stay copacetic!

You Will Need
+ a small glass bottle or container with a cork or cover
+ some candy (your boss's favorite, if possible)
+ a picture of or signature from the boss
+ some white rose petals

The Spell
At the full moon, put all of the items in the glass bottle, open it so the moonlight falls inside the jar, and say:

Selene Fair
With silver hair
Fill with sweetness
This friendship charm
May (name) who's above me
Never bring harm.

Hold the bottle in both hands and close it up,
thinking intently of your boss, and say:

By rose and sweets
And image of thee
Remember to always
Look kindly toward me
Selene by thy will
So may it be!

Keep this little charm in your desk (hidden, of course!)
and you will stay on this supervisor's good side!

The New Employee Spell

So there's fresh "meat" in the office, hmm? It's always a karmic connection, a spin on the human resources roulette wheel. Will he be nice? It never really changes from kindergarten: People you work and/or play with are either nice or mean. Isn't it amazing how simple some things are? You just want a coworker who "plays well with others." Try this spell out whenever a new person suddenly becomes a coworker to determine the truth: Is he or she friend or foe? This'll let you know! Reveal the new guy's true feathers and see what's up!

You Will Need
+ a peacock feather
+ some spring water

The Spell
At midnight on a Wednesday, take the feather in your right
hand and spin it around clockwise three times. Say:

FEATHER OF TRUTH
SHOW THE REAL
TRUTH OF (name)
AND WHAT THEY FEEL!
THEmis!

Sprinkle it with spring water, and say:

CLEAR THE mOUTH, THE HAND, AND EYE
SHOW UP EVERY TRUTH AND LIE
FRIEND OR FOE
LET mE KNOW!
THEmis!

Go to the office or working area of the new employee.
Point the feather to the four directions and then hide
it somewhere, whispering:

THEMIS!
BY EACH DIRECTION
GIVE ME JOY
OR PROTECTION!

You'll soon find out whether you have a Jekyll or Hyde coworker; this little truth spell will reveal his or her true colors.

If they are good, all is well and you'll make a pal. If not, get the feather back from its hiding place and keep it at your desk, and this person will do you no harm. That's the Truth!

PHOTOCOPIER HOG SPELL

You just need one copy, right? But noooooooooo . . .
Mr. or Ms. Copy-by-the-Ton has decided to copy (it seems)
the Webster's dictionary, in triplicate, collated. And is this the
first time? Noooooo . . . Okay, so are you going to sit there
and whine about it? I didn't think so! Roll up the
magic sleeves and toss this puppy! With this spell the
copy machine situation will become saner and you
can stop wasting time on it and get back to wasting
time on stuff *you* want to pretend to do!

YOU WILL NEED
+ a copy this machine has made
+ brown marker

THE SPELL

As the sun is setting, take the paper and with the
brown marker, write the following sentence in
a circle around the paper:

USE WHEN YOU NEED . . . NOT WITH GREED . . .
WORK WITH SPEED!

In the middle draw this rune:

Then, make four copies of this on the machine, fold them up,
and place them under the four legs of the copier or inside the
copier. Leave the original in the copier for a moment, saying:

HELP ONLY THOSE WHO NEED
REPEL THOSE WITH GREED
PUSH THE SLOW WITH SPEED
PRECIOUS IS THE GIFT OF WORD
LET THIS SPELL NOW BE HEARD!

Tear up the original, put it into the recycling bin, and say:

> SO MAY IT BE
> COPIER BE FREE!

Go forth and copy with joy and abandon and,
dare I say it, a semblance of efficiency?

SUPREME OFFICE SUPPLIES PROTECTION SPELL

Need your stapler? Well, just look in your drawer and . . . it's gone! Well, tape will work, your dispenser is right . . . oh, someone "borrowed" it, *again!* Tacks? Pens? Gee, some people sure have sticky fingers! Either that or your items have formed a secret office supply escape plan and are even now on their way to the planet of the lost scissors. Tired of supplying everyone who "just needs it for a minute please"? Do this little spell on your stuff and your things will stick to your desk like glue and snap back like rubber bands if they are borrowed!

YOU WILL NEED
+ a small knife
+ a magnet (a refrigerator magnet will do)
+ an indelible pen

THE SPELL

At the new moon, use the knife to scratch a
five-pointed star into the magnet, saying:

BY RULER WAND AND SCISSORS' KNIFE
TABLE OF EARTH AND COFFEE CUP OF LIFE
SPIRIT OF WORK AND POWER OF PLAY
ALL THAT IS MINE WILL STAY STAY STAY!
INSTRUMENTUM DETINERE!

Now draw a star on the bottom of each of your
office supplies and then rub the magnet on
each of them three times, saying:

ATTRACT AND HOLD
ATTRACT AND SEAL
SEAL TO ME
DO NOT GO FREE
LET NOBODY STEAL!
VULCAN MAKE REAL!

Place the magnet in your top drawer or leave it on
your desk. Your stuff will not roam far or for long.
If something does go missing, rub the magnet and
repeat the verse—it will turn up!

Power Meeting Spell to Get What You Want

Oh my! A big meeting looms and you need to project an aura of
power and invincibility. You need help, right? You need things
to go your way. You need the deal to come off or the client to
be completely impressed or that big decision to be made in
your favor. You know exactly what you want so badly you can
taste it! This little spell will raise your energy and help success
materialize. Get decked out: a new haircut, a wicked smile, a
little deep breathing . . . and this little charm. Look out, world!

You Will Need
+ frankincense oil (Fire oil)
+ patchouli oil (Earth oil)

The Spell
When you are alone, just after dawn on the big day, put a
bit of the Fire and Earth oil on the center of your forehead
(your "third eye") as you are looking in the mirror.

See fire around you as you stand on solid earth. Say:

> POWER INSIDE
> POWER OUT
> POWER AWAKEN
> THROUGHOUT AND ABOUT

Place a little of both oils on your hands and
rub them together. Say:

> POWER EARTH
> MY WILL GIVE BIRTH
> I'LL GET WHAT I NEED
> I SHALL SUCCEED!

Clap your hands once and cup them; close your eyes.
Visualize what you need to have fall into your hands. Clasp
them together and then open your eyes. Vrooooooom!
Go to that meeting and get what you want!

SHUTTING DOWN A
NASTY COWORKER HEX

You say hi and get a dirty look. A "good morning" gets you a
snide comment. You try to be nice—well, most of the time—
but this *&%@# just wants to be nasty. Who knows why?
Maybe you remind this twit of a past schoolmate who was
also smarter and more talented? Well, not your problem—
except that this one keeps sending the bad vibes and making
life unpleasant! Freeze this nasty little bug fast and be
free of the evil eye! Here's how:

YOU WILL NEED
+ a small something this person has touched
+ an indelible blue pen
+ a paper cup and water

THE SPELL

On the item the nasty one has touched, draw a single line
with the blue pen and say:

Iis
Ice
Hold them
Tight
Feet
Then legs
Chest and
Head
Freeze the mouth
And fill
With dread
Runa-iis
Bind the bad
Still the one
Who makes me mad
Iis!

Then put this crumpled paper in the cup, fill with water, and place in the back of your freezer. As it freezes, see your nemesis freeze. Now they are as removed from you as an iceberg!

In the spring, if you have pity on them, let the cup thaw out in the sun . . . but that is strictly up to you!

GET THE DAY OFF SPELL

You want—no, *need*—a day off desperately. Maybe it is
a mental health day, or maybe you're thinking of that
treasured wild lunch date or a new hairdresser or tickets
to a good game or a hot concert . . . you need a day off! Toss
this one across the plate and watch your boss swing for it!

YOU WILL NEED
+ some lavender oil
+ a calendar
+ a small piece of carnelian stone
(you can get this at a mineral store)

THE SPELL
First, place some of the lavender oil, just a dab, on the
calendar on the day you want off. Then put some on
yourself and on the carnelian, saying:

AIR ABOVE
AIR BELOW
CIRCLE IN FAST
CIRCLE 'BOUT SLOW
COME TO ME
THEN LET ME GO
GRANT ME FREETIME
MAKE IT SO!
EUROS!

Place the carnelian in your pocket and then, after lunch,
go to your boss and ask. You'll get your day off,
and maybe more! Keep that stone around;
you may need another day off soon!

SELL SELL SELL SPELL

Even if you're not in sales (but especially if you are!), you
will have to sell something to someone sometime, right?
I mean, that is what makes the capitalist world go 'round.
So the world is divided between sellers and buyers, and
for now you want to be a seller, but not just a so-so seller,
a *super* seller! This little spell will rocket your numbers
and move that product pronto!

YOU WILL NEED
* a whole cinnamon stick
* a small knife
* some orange thread

THE SPELL

Under a full moon, gather your items together. Carve this "P" rune into the cinnamon stick with the knife. Say:

ARROW OF WORD
SIGN AND DEED
HIT EYES
MIND AND HEART
SO ALL FOLLOW
MY LEAD
SO ALL WILL BUY
ALL THAT I NEED!
Wunjo!

Wrap the orange thread around the stick twenty-three times, each time saying:

FIX THE SPELL
SELL WELL!

Tie the thread off three times and circle yourself
with the finished charm, saying:

> WUNJO MAKE IT WELL
> FIX NOW THE SPELL
> SELL SELL SELL!

Keep this in your coat pocket or purse. When ready to sell,
chew a bit off the end of the stick and repeat the last verse—
the money will come flying in, O cinnamon breath!

GET A GOOD BOSS SPELL

Your supervisor has flown the corporate coop and a new boss
is on the way . . . will he/she be Glinda the Good Witch or
The Wicked Witch of the East? We are all, of course, at the
hands of capitalist fates, but a little spell can stack the odds
a bit so you'll get a boss definitely better than Attila the Hun,
maybe even a human being! Miracles can happen—here's how:

YOU WILL NEED
+ a piece of yellow paper
+ a nice vase filled with water
+ a pinch of sugar
+ a yellow long-stem rose that is just opening

THE SPELL
A few days before a full moon, on a Friday, get out the yellow
paper and chat with your fellow employees. Tell them that

they should all make a wish for a cool boss and have them
give you specific traits you want the new boss to have,
like: honest, fair, funny, flexible . . . and normal!

Write these carefully on the yellow paper.
When done, hide it away until that night.

At that time, if possible, go into the future boss's office
(or yours if you can't get to that office) with the water-
filled vase, the paper, the sugar, and the rose.

Sprinkle sugar in the vase and around the office
in a clock wise circle, saying:

CRYSTALS OF PROSPERITY
COME AND SET THE OFFICE FREE
FROM ALL NEGATIVITY
SHRING SHRING SHRING
SO MAY IT BE!

Tightly wrap the paper around the end of the rose stem, then hold it with both hands and say:

GREAT GOLDEN RAY
BRING US A FRIEND
ONE JUST AND HONEST
AND KIND TO THE END
SHRING!

Place the wrapped stem into the vase. The rose should thus stand in the water of the vase and the paper should be under the water. If at all possible, leave this rose in the office of the future boss, or at least near it.

Then wait. There *are* good bosses out there (really!), and you're about to get one!

"My Job Would Be Perfect
If It Only . . ." Spell

Finally you've got the job of your dreams and it is fine with
you if you never leave it. There is only one tiny little problem
that could be cleared up if only you had a magic wand—then,
poof!, the special problem would disappear. The problem
might be the hours, location, a bad procedure, or some task
that you would prefer to land on someone else. Dump the
little glitch that stops the job from being absolutely perfect.
No matter what it is, here is a handy catch-all make-the-job-
better spell where you can create the reality that you want.
The only limit is your imagination!

You Will Need
+ a blue pen
+ stationery with your company's logo on it
(or something similar)
+ jasmine oil
+ a pink candle
+ matches

The Spell
Under a full moon, draw a large circle with the blue pen
on the paper and hold it up to the moon. Put some
jasmine oil around this drawn circle, a little on your
neck, and a bit on the candle, saying:

By the circle of the moon
By my will to make things right
Fill my spell and cast it soon
I call down the secret moonlight
Tua khonsu!

Write on the stationery, around the inside rim of the circle,
what it is that you want to change. "I need and will get

more . . ." or something like that; fill in the blank with your desire. Spend time with this—no scribbling or messy penmanship. Really concentrate on what it is you desire.
Then light the pink candle and say:

CANDLE OF DESIRE, BY FLAME, TALLOW, AND WICK
GIVE ME MY HEART'S DESIRE AND
GIVE IT TO ME QUICK
I KNOW WHAT I NEED AND I KNOW WHAT I MISS
TO HEED MY WISH, I SEAL IT WITH A KISS!

Read out loud what you desire; shout it out until your neighbors hear you! Kiss the paper right in the center as you would kiss a lover, fill it with your desire, and see it come true!

Then, using the candle, burn the paper and collect the ashes. Let the candle burn down completely, then toss the ashes into a body of water.

Wear the jasmine oil every day for at least a week or until your problem has vanished or transformed. Repeat as needed!

A Spell to Influence Others' Dreams

Midnight, the witching hour, is when most of us do our best spells! When you wake up do you ever wonder why you dreamed about a certain person? Someone you have not thought of in years who calls you the next morning out of the blue? This is true magic, subtle motion and movement that can change your life. Dreams are an easy way to enter the magic world where things can be influenced. This is a sneaky little spell that is a family favorite passed down through generations and taught to me by my grandfather. I now will tell you how to influence others in their dream state! If you decide to influence others in this way, some surprises may come out of the blue for you!

You Will Need

+ a "lucky candle" (this is a large candle in a cylindrical glass container with many lucky symbols all over the glass)
+ matches
+ the business card(s) of those you want to influence
+ gardenia oil

The Spell

At midnight, on any night of the week, light the candle and tape the cards around it. (These candles are in glass so there is little chance of a fire hazard.) Put the oil in a vessel or special cup (I use a seashell). Then when you are ready, rub some oil on the cards, your temples, and on the candle. Light the candle and say:

> Sweet dreams to those who dream
> Of very special nighttime things
> Music, prosperity, and creativity
> Now the spell brings
> Dream of us tonight, today

MAY THE WORLD OF THE NIGHT
MEET THE WORLD OF THE DAY.
IN THE MORNING YOU WAKE FROM YOUR SLEEP
GOOD THOUGHTS OF ME YOU'LL FOREVER KEEP!

Visualize what it is that you want to have happen, how you
wish to influence these people, and then whisper their
names and yours and what you want them to dream of.
Blow the candle out and put it away. This is your secret
dream candle—use it only when you want to influence
others' dreams. Be respectful with this spell and use
your candle only occasionally and nicely! Dreams
have a way of returning. Pleasant dreams!

The Anti-Oops Spell
(Charm for a Second Chance)

Now, wasn't that a hoot? At the time it was funny and the whole office was laughing and that just gave a little more fuel for the fire. So, of course, you got a little louder and then your boss walked by the open door and there you were, thinking the astonished look on your coworkers' faces was because you were so entertaining. Unfortunately, you were doing a great job of impersonating the boss in a very unflattering manner (or some other idiotic thing), you turned around, and there was your boss—and he was not smiling. *Oops!* Or maybe you sent the wrong e-mail or got caught at a nasty Web site or accidentally insulted the boss's bratty kid. You did not lose your job (this time), but now you are an office outcast. This little spell will get you back in favor after even the worst faux pas, blooper, or stupid blunder!

You Will Need
+ a bowl (not plastic) of pure water
+ a stone of rose quartz
+ something belonging to your boss
(or the higher-up you offended)
+ a stick of your favorite flowery incense

The Spell
Take the bowl of water and put the rose quartz in it.
Then add the object from your boss. Circle the lit incense
around the bowl in a spiral clockwise motion and say:

SEA, RIVER, LAKE, STREAM, OCEAN
WASH AWAY WHAT I HAVE SPOKEN
MY DEEDS WERE WRONG, WHAT I DID WAS MEAN
WASH AWAY WHAT I DID AND WHAT WAS SEEN
SEA, RIVER, LAKE, STREAM, OCEAN
I ERASE MY FAULT WITH THE SPIRAL MOTION
NIHIL EST, NIHIL EST, NIHIL EST!

Extinguish the incense in the center of the water, and as the water ripples, so your blunder will disappear. Then, dump the water at the base of a tree and bury the object from the boss or put it back (depending on what it is!). Take the rose quartz and put it on your desk to keep bad reputation away. And try to keep your yap shut a little more often.

Signing-off Hex

You should always listen to your intuition! Kicking yourself
now, right? You had a deep-down feeling that this was not
the right person to do business with, and that nagging feeling
never went away. You knew better, but the opportunity
seemed right, or he was recommended by an associate or he
just "seemed nice." So you signed a contract or made a deal
or formed a relationship with this idiot and it was a mistake!
What is one to do? No matter how screwed you feel, nothing
is worse than to allow problems with people like this to continue. This is a spell to hex this person and to dissolve the
relationship by making him go away without so much as a peep!

You Will Need
+ one white candle
+ matches
+ five pushpins
+ a red pen
+ a self-stick note

THE SPELL

On a Saturday night at midnight, near the dark of the moon, light the candle while naming your hex-associate five times. Then, stick the candle with each of the five pushpins and say each time:

ADVANTAGE YOU TOOK OF ME
I WAS BLIND BUT NOW I SEE
FRIEND TURNED TO FOE
LET ME GO!
FINITATUS EST!

While you are poking pins into the candle, visualize that your associate will soon be your ex-associate. While doing this, say:

I LEARNED MY LESSON
THERE IS NO TRUST, WE'RE THROUGH
WITH THIS SPELL I AM RELEASED FROM YOU.
FINITATUS EST!

Then take the red pen and the self-stick note.

With the red pen, sign your name and the name of the other person on the self-stick note. Rip the paper so the names are divided and say:

CRUEL AND TREACHEROUS NEVERMORE
OUR BOND IS BROKEN
BEGINNING NOW AND FOREVER MORE!
FINITATUS EST!

Burn his half of the note and blow the ashes out a window or door. Keep your half. Burn the candle down until the pushpins fall out, then blow it out, saying

FINITATUS EST!

Toss all the debris out except one pushpin. Make sure your ex-pal gets this or that it is left in his or her office. And another one bites the dust! Next time, think twice before signing on the dotted line!

Peaceful Office Spell

Fantasy time: It would be nice if you came in to work one day and everyone at your job was civil, the work flowed with professional ease, everyone did their job with efficiency and satisfaction, and (what the heck, it's a fantasy!) the lunch was catered! But hey, this is work, and none of us would actually be here if we weren't getting paid, right? Still, the office tension might be heading into overload. Maybe the bad feelings are a bit too heavy lately? Fights? Misunderstandings that ended up as disasters? General everyone-is-nuts-today vibe in the air? Well, we all want to have that perfect-job fantasy come true, and this spell will probably not do *all* that, but it will calm things down, bring a little peace, and cool the tempers and touchy egos in that raspy office.

It's a start! Give peace a chance.

You Will Need
+ three fern fronds
+ white lilies in a clear vase

The Spell
At night, when no one is around (or very early in the morning), walk in a clockwise direction around the office shaking the fern fronds, saying:

Banish anger red
By power of green
Hate, tension, and grief
And all evil unseen!

Then walk counterclockwise and brush all the "trouble spots" with the fern fronds: the quarrelers' desks, places of high tension, meeting rooms, and so on. As you do, say:

Tout tout
Around and about
All evil out all evil out!

When done, toss the fronds into the trash.

Then take up the lilies in the vase and walk clockwise around the office, into every problem room, saying over and over:

Omni pax
Omnia felix
Omnia fortuna!

Place the vase on your desk and say:

Peace, joy, and prosperity
Around this place
So may it be!

Ah! What a relief to be able just to work again!

Spell to Merit a Merit Raise

Hey, you are a hot worker, supreme in most every way (where you're lacking, well, that is what underlings are for, right?). So you deserve a merit raise today! Right? Right! Affirmations are swell ("I deserve it and, gosh darn it, I'm gonna get it!"), but if you want the deal to really go down, throw in a little magic and make the powers that be stand up and take notice of your excellent work!

You Will Need
+ a small gold candle
+ matches
+ a small ring, necklace, earring, or nose ring
made of gold or gold plated
+ a little saffron
+ some cinnamon

THE SPELL

On a sunny day, at noon, find a sunny place where you can't be seen (an open window ledge is fine) and light the candle while looking up at the sun (briefly!). Then say:

SOL invincus
DESCEND TO FLAME
THINGS NOW OKAY
DON'T STAY THE SAME
BRING TO ME
WEALTH AND FAME
SOL invincus
BY THIS FLAME!

With your right hand, hold the gold object over the flame, while with your left hand, sprinkle a pinch of saffron over the flame. It will burn in a few sparks. Make sure the ring is touched by these sparks but don't get burned! Say:

FILL WITH POWER
NOW'S THE HOUR
I SET IN MOTION
MY PROMOTION
BY WILL AND LOVE
I'LL RISE ABOVE
SOL INVINCUS!

Touch the gold item to the flame three times, rub some cinnamon into it, and then put it on. Let the candle burn to nothing (watching it carefully!). Wear your gold as much as you can at the office and keep rubbing saffron into it every day. After that, you'd better start checking out some nifty new things you're going to buy with that extra moola . . .

Commuter Safety Spell

Some people say work is hell; I think not. Work is purgatory (after thirty years, you get to heaven or retirement, which-ever comes first). But commuting—commuting is indeed hell. If you are not dodging crazed truckers, cell phone–chatting yuppies, or girls doing their makeup while changing lanes at 70 mph, you have to confront the dreaded traffic jams. *Or* you get to slam bodies with sweaty don't-you-wish-everyone-used-Dial lemmings on the bus or *(gasp!)* the subway. *Sigh.* For what? To get to work?! It is all so unfair. Still, no matter what, one wants to make it there and back in one piece, with no problems, right? This spell is made to protect you from deranged drivers, weirdos, or seriously offensive people. And you can give these charms as birthday gifts!

YOU WILL NEED
+ matches
+ a sprig of rosemary
+ two small pieces of cardboard or stiff paper—
one white, one red
+ glue
+ a black marker
+ a piece of white string or thread

THE SPELL
On a Wednesday, early in the morning, assemble all
the items. Face east. Burn a little of the rosemary
and circle about the area eight times, saying:

HERMES LEYVERTICES
ON THE EIGHT WINDS
COME O PLEASE
ALL BE SAFE WHO CARRY THESE
COME O COME
LEYVERTICES

Laying the two cardboard pieces in the shape of a diamond on top of each other, glue them together with the sprig of rosemary between them.

On the red side, draw this rune:

On the white side, draw this rune:

At the top, make a small hole and put the thread or string through it and knot it three times. Say:

> By the three and the one
> By the star and the sun
> Protect me on my way I go
> Avert all harm

MAY I FLOW
WHERE I WILL EVERY DAY
WITH GREAT JOY ON MY WAY!

Clap eight times and hang the charm from your
car mirror or carry it with you.

Happy commuting!

Spell to Increase Profits

We can all use more money, right? And if you have a small (or big) business, you need to—all together now—*maximize profits!*—hopefully in a nice way, right? But still, there is no harm in asking the universe for a rising profit curve, and if you ask right, the universe might give it to you!

You Will Need
+ a symbol of the company (a logo on stationery is fine)
+ a green cup (not plastic)
+ a small piece of jade
+ a handful of silver coins (dimes are fine)
+ a stick of patchouli incense
+ matches

The Spell
At the new moon, place the logo into the green cup,
place the jade on it, and say:

Business rooted
Here on earth
Fill with profit
Cup of rebirth
Cornucopia est!

Now, take the cup to each of the four directions of the room
and again to the center. Each time say the following and
drop silver coins into the cup onto the stone and logo:

Profit fall like rain
Fill my cup with gain
Cornucopia est!

The cup should be about half full of coins.
Then stick the incense in it and light it, saying:

> CORNUCOPIA DEA
> HEAR MY PLEA
> AS THIS CUP IS FULL
> SO MAY THE COFFERS BE
> INCREASE MY PROFIT
> BRING IT TO ME!

Let it burn out, then mix the ashes with the coins and keep
this cup on your desk or someplace connected with your
business. Every time you receive some new business, cash
the check and put a silver coin from it into the cup and
repeat the last verse—your profits will continue to increase!

A Spell to Keep Baby Pictures at Bay

Who doesn't like babies? Most people like them even more if they produce them—go figure. They are all cute, but they're sure not all pretty and, let's face it, it isn't like kids are a new invention, right? Yet new parents (not to mention proud pet owners, obsessive gardeners, Kodak travelers, etc.) love, love, love to show off pictures. A few pictures are nice; many could, on a very boring work day, be interesting. But too many . . . well, we have all felt like a fox in a bear trap when cornered by a friendly soul with a pile of pictures, right? You could gnaw your leg off to escape (don't— your HMO doesn't cover it) or you could do this little spell to deflect the photoholic to another poor soul.

You Will Need
+ an old bad photo of nothing (one of those thumb shots!)
+ two pins

THE SPELL

At the dark of the moon, at work (wherever you are photo-accosted the most) take up the photo and say the name of the photo stalker nine times while rubbing the photo between your hands, then say:

ALL LOVE YOUR PICTURES
BUT NOT SO OFTEN
THE AMOUNT YOU INFLICT
NOW MUST LESSEN
SHOW ME THEM BRIEFLY
LESS HERE IS MORE
YOU'RE AVERTED IF TOO MUCH
NO MORE WILL YOU BORE!
AVERTUS AVERTUM AVERTI!
NO MORE PICTURES
SO MAY IT BE!

Stick the pin into the photo to form an "X" and visualize
the photo fiend being driven away if his or her photo
rap goes on too long. Then toss the picture.

The photo king or queen should back off
real soon . . . whew!

I Want an Award Spell

Employee awards are often lame and silly, unfair and dumb—
except when you win one, right? When that happens, of
course, you deserve it—richly—for putting up with . . .
well, I don't have to tell *you* what you put up with, right?
So whether it's Employee of the Year, the In Service Award,
the Secretaries Day Present, or whatever, when you want—
no, *need*—to be recognized for being the unbelievably
patient, swell employee that you are, this spell should
enlighten the deciders of such things and get you that
spotlight (or gift certificate) that you really, really do deserve!

You Will Need
+ a piece of light blue paper
+ some cedar- or pine-scented oil
+ matches

The Spell

On the piece of paper, write out an award for yourself
that is appropriate and possible to get at your job. Make
it really nice and fancy. Write your name prominently in
the center after "Awarded To." Place some of the pine oil
on the corners of the paper and on your name, then
dab some on your neck and heart, and say:

Tyr tyr tyr!
Power of pine
And sky so fair
Bring me a gift
By earth and by air
Bring me an award
I so richly deserve
For the work I do
With wit, skill, and verve!
Tyr of plenty
So may it be
Bring my award
Award it to me!

Then burn the paper while visualizing the award ceremony. After that, bury the ashes at the base of a pine tree while repeating the rhyme above.

Say the rhyme one more time the next morning when you dab on some more pine oil before going to work. Keep wearing the oil for a week or so, then clear a spot off your mantel or wall for that new award.

The Big Expense Account Spell

All meaningless talk of efficiency and the bottom line
and tight budgets aside, we know that the Holy Grail
of a decent job is the expense account, right? If you'd
like one, but don't have one, or you have one but it's
not enough, this little spell should put the gleam back
in that company smile and put that gold card back
into your hot little think-I'll-have-the-lobster wallet!
Always remember this mantra, however:
Keep the receipt, keep the receipt, keep the receipt . . .

You Will Need
✦ a company expense form or a copy of one
✦ a pen or pencil
✦ forty-four pennies
✦ some green thread

THE SPELL
On a Thursday at sunset, during a waxing
moon, go to the ocean, a lake, or a river.
Fill in your name on the expense form and
enter how much you want to be able to
spend in the "Total" box. Draw four concentric circles on the
paper with a big Jupiter symbol in the center. Then say:

CHARGE IT CHARGE IT
JOVE ENLARGE IT
COMPANY CASH FLOW
WHEREVER I GO
COME FAST NOT SLOW
JOVE MAY IT GROW!

Drop the forty-four pennies into the center of it and say:

FOUR BY FOUR
MAY IT BECOME MORE
COINS EXPAND
ON WATER AND LAND!

Wrap it all up and then wrap the thread around it
to hold it together, saying:

> MONEY INCREASE
> BOUND TO ME
> BRINGING ME CREDIT
> AND PROSPERITY!

See your expense account, big and fat, fall into your lap.
Then toss it into the water and say:

> JOVE TAKE IT
> JOVE MAKE IT
> JOVE SEE IT BE
> BY JOVE
> MAY IT COME TO ME!
> AND GROW LIKE A TREE!

Your efforts to get or enlarge that expense account will soon
bear fruit if you make the effort to shake that money tree!

Hex to Get Rid of the Office Jerk

We can all cope with office hissy-fits, computer disasters, grandstanding coworkers, and insane bosses—but is there ever a reason to get mean? Yet there is always an office jerk. Some people, even when not stressed to the max (like you), just like humiliating people and causing pain. Grrrr! Some of the things that office snake does to coworkers, or even to *you*, should never happen! This is a little psychic cleaning spell to make the nasty person beat it or get kinder (unlikely with these types)! Remember: This is not for simply unpleasant people or sometimes rough people, this is for those seriously sick nasties! Show this spell to your fellow decent coworkers and have them do it too! Call it a psychic posse if you will. An office is like the Wild West, and sometimes you just have to take justice into your own hands.

YOU WILL NEED
+ some red pepper
+ some vinegar in a small cup
+ a black feather you found

THE SPELL
On the dark of the moon, mix the pepper
into the cup of vinegar and say:

FIRE OF ANGER
BILE OF HATE
I CHARGE THEE BEGONE
BEFORE IT'S TOO LATE
HEKATE HEKATE
MAKE IT SO
DARK WIND ARISE
MAKE (NAME) GO!

Pour the mixture over the feather and say:

> HOT AND BITTER
> I CHARGE THEE
> FROM YOUR POWER
> EVIL ONE FLEE!

Dry the feather out overnight and the next day drop the feather on the a-hole's desk, cubicle, or chair, and mutter:

> JUSTICE NOW
> DART FLY FREE
> EXPEL THIS VIPER
> SO MAY IT BE!
> LUTIS NITRA!

Never admit to leaving the feather and never touch it again. The nasty one will soon be packing.

Launching a New Project Spell

Beginnings, the ancients say, are the most crucial part of any undertaking. Anyone who has forgotten their plane ticket or forgotten to fill a gas tank will agree! Any project at work, no matter what it might be, could be really important to your company and, more importantly, to you and your infamous career! To make magically sure that you're getting the project off on the right foot (to prosperity and fame!), do this little charm—and you're off!

You Will Need
+ a bit of salt
+ a stick of sandalwood incense
+ matches
+ a white carnation

THE SPELL

On a Monday, with the moon waxing, go to the place
where the project will begin and toss the grains of salt
to the four directions, saying:

> GAM! ALL OBSTRUCTIONS
> AND BLOCKS AWAY BLOW
> SUCCESS IS ASSURED
> ALL BARRIERS AWAY FLOW!

Light the incense and circle the focus of the
project three times, saying:

> GAM! WINDS OF SUCCESS
> FLOW HERE TONIGHT
> GATHER ALL GOOD
> AND FOCUS THE LIGHT
> LET ALL WORK OUT WELL
> LET ALL TURN OUT RIGHT!

Place the white carnation on the appropriate place and say:

> GAM! HERE IS CENTERED
> AND GOOD LUCK SEALED
> WITH WILL AND HARD WORK
> SUCCESS BE REVEALED!
> GAM GAM GAM!

Put out the incense and leave the white carnation.
Later, hang it somewhere and let it dry. Make sure
you keep it safe until the project succeeds!

Spell for a Positive Transfer

If you're tired of your position and you'd like a transfer, or if a transfer has—how can I say this delicately—been offered to you in a most insistent manner, then this is the spell for you! Whether we wish joyfully to leap into a new existence or we are being thrust off a plank at saber point, there is grace in adapting with style and success. This spell will help insure a successful and prosperous transfer. Never fear the new! Something good is waiting just around the corner!

You Will Need
+ a small cloth bag
+ some beans
+ a flower from an office arrangement
+ an acorn

THE SPELL

At the new moon (or close to it) take all these items
to your work area and lay them out on your desk.
Place the beans in the bag and say:

> HERE IS THE WORK
> I PLANTED IN THIS PLACE
> I TAKE IT WITH ME
> THERE IS NO DISGRACE
> MY EFFORT WAS GOOD
> MY EFFORT WAS FINE
> I TAKE BACK MY POWER
> FOR IT IS ALL MINE!

Place the flower from the office in the bag and say:

> HERE IS THE LOVE
> I GAINED FROM THIS PLACE
> I TAKE IT WITH ME
> THERE IS NO DISGRACE
> THE FUN AND CAMARADERIE

I GAINED HERE WAS GOOD
I'LL KEEP IT WITH ME
AS FOREVER I SHOULD!

Place the acorn into the pouch and say:

HERE IS THE SKILL
I GAINED FROM THIS PLACE
NOW IT GROWS IN ME
THERE IS NO DISGRACE
EVERY DAY GAVE ME KNOWLEDGE
AND SPECIAL WISDOM
I'LL NURTURE AND SPREAD IT
FROM ME WILL IT COME!

Tighten up the bag and swing it around your head clockwise
three times while you visualize all the energy you planted in
this place flowing into the bag. Keep it in your desk and
when you leave, take it with you in your pocket.

After you are transferred, bring the bag first thing
to your new work area, open the top of the bag
a little, and put it in your desk, saying:

> MY WORK, LOVE, AND SKILL
> THEY GROW IN ME STILL
> HERE I'M NOW PLANTED
> MAY ALL THAT I WISH FOR
> BE HERE GRANTED!

Kick back, relax, do your best, and get out there and
have fun! New beginnings are a turn-on; enjoy!

Love My Office Potluck Spell

So, it's time to bring something yummy into the office to show everyone how wonderful you are. Maybe it's a potluck? Maybe a birthday bash? A retiring? Who knows, but food is part of it and you want to make your dish count just a little bit more. A little magic mixed in with the sauce and salt can add that extra glamour that will make people think more kindly of you—how could it hurt? They'll love your dish and afterward, they'll all love you just a little bit more as well. *Bon appétit!* (Works for everything but Jell-O salad . . .)

You Will Need
+ honey
+ a little fresh mint
+ sesame seeds
+ whatever dish you are making

THE SPELL
As you're making the dish, first add a bit of honey, saying:

POWER OF SUN AND FLOWER AND BEE
WINDS OF SUMMER AND LEAVES OF TREE
MAY EVERYTHING I DO AND SAY
BE SEEN AS SWEET AND GENTLE PLAY!

Then add a little chopped-up mint, saying:

POWER OF EARTH AND GREEN AND FIRE
STRONG FRAGRANT OILS AND JOYFUL DESIRE
MAY EVERYTHING I DO AND SAY
BE SEEN AS INSPIRED AND CREATIVE PLAY!

Sprinkle some sesame seeds into the dish and say:

POWER OF LIFE AND WEALTH AND FUN
PROSPERITY, LOYALTY, AND LIFE BEGUN
MAY EVERYTHING I DO AND SAY
BE SEEN AS LOVING AND DEDICATED PLAY!

When the dish is done, trace a triangle over it
three times and say:

WITH EVERY BITE
YOU WILL SEE
SOMEONE LOVING, LOYAL, AND FREE
YOU WILL KINDLY LOOK UPON ME
AS I WILL
SO MAY IT BE!

POWER LUNCH/DINNER SPELL

You're in a somewhat minor panic. Maybe it is lunch with
the boss or dinner with a very important client or a buffet
with the visiting vice president of the company. You have
to be graceful, witty, and charming, and make that person
or people like you and listen to you, right? If you can
avoid dumping the soup in your lap, breaking the
crystal, or sneezing between courses, this spell will
help you have a very successful business meal!
And the service should be better, too.

YOU WILL NEED
+ some powdered ginger
+ some ground cinnamon
+ some ground nutmeg
+ cloth napkin
+ small container

THE SPELL

Before the appointment, mix the spices on a white napkin
and leave it open to the sunlight for a full day, if possible.
As you lay the mixture out, say:

FIRE OF SUN, OF EARTH AND AIR
FIRE OF MY WILL AND MY SPIRIT FAIR
BY SPICES AND SUNLIGHT-FIRE
MAKE REAL MY EVERY DESIRE
İGNIS SPIRITUS!

Then put the mix into a small container and keep it with you.

At the meal, sprinkle a bit of the spice mix on your hair
and lightly rub it on both your hands. If possible, put
a very small pinch of it in your dinner partner's food,
discreetly! (Try and make sure he or she is not allergic
to any of the spices; a sick client is not a good client.)
As you do this (or just when you shake spice-rubbed
hands with your associate) mutter under your breath:

> By my flame of desire
> By will and spirit's fire
> Feel me sparkle
> Feel me shine
> Feel me to be
> A business partner divine!

You will literally dazzle your dinner companions and leave a sparkle in their eyes. At the end of the meal they will be absolutely charmed by your bright spirit!

Hex for Keeping Free of Office Politics

What's more vicious than a rabid Doberman? What causes more carnage than a T-rex? What is as venomous as a rattlesnake and as poisonous as a scorpion? That's right! Office politics! An office torn apart by in-fighting and backbiting and jockeying for power is an ugly sight, like a corporate Sarajevo. If you are still sane and not infected with the madness, your number-one goal should be to stay clear. When the political mortars and shrapnel start flying, dig a protective foxhole with this spell.

You Will Need
+ some dark blue yarn
+ a nice healthy maple tree

The Spell
At midnight, about three days before a full moon,
tie the piece of yarn to a branch of the tree. Say:

> CALM YOU ARE
> SO CALM MAKE ME
> I'M SHELTERED
> BY THE BRANCHES OF THEE
> NOTHING CAN HARM ME
> FOR I AM A TREE!
> SYLVIA DEA
> SO MAY IT BE!

Three days later, come back and take most of the yarn.
Leave a bit tied to the tree. Tie the yarn around your left
wrist (or ankle if you need to be more discreet) and
visualize being protected from all the nastiness at
work by a tree of blue energy, saying:

I AM SHELTERED BY THE TREE
NO HARM NOR ILL
SHALL BEFALL ME
BY THE SYLVAN POWERS FREE
AS I WILL, SO MAY IT BE!

This will keep you snug and rockabye-baby-in-the-treetop-safe, but your bough won't break and you won't fall! You'll weather the political storms and come out smelling like a rose!

Antivirus and Anticrash
Computer Protection Spell

So, you need that report right away for a critical meeting?
No problem! Just call it up on the computer and . . . what's
this? Error? Crash? Black screen? Laughing faces? Ahhh!
And you thought high tech was supposed to make life easier,
didn't you? Well, after you've serviced your computer, gotten
antivirus software installed, and so on, there is still this
mysterious possibility of something really evil happening
to your I-need-this-so-badly computer, right? Keep the
cyber forces of darkness at bay with this spell!

You Will Need
+ your computer
+ a little time
+ a small crystal

THE SPELL

At the full moon, start your computer, open a new
text document, and write the following:

S	a	t	o	r
A	r	e	p	o
T	e	n	e	t
O	p	e	r	a
R	o	t	a	s

With this on the screen, repeat these words three times
while circling the computer three times with the
crystal. Place the crystal on the computer,
save the document as "Avert," and say:

BY CROOK AND WHEEL
VOICE AND WORD
THIS CHARM TO AVERT
IS NOW HEARD
AUDIRE!

Store the document in your hard drive. Keep the crystal near or on the computer. When cyber evil threatens, stroke the crystal and repeat the spell—but not when your boss is looking. Some people just don't understand.

HEAVY PROTECTION FROM SALESMEN SPELL

"Hiiiiiiiii there!" Big sincere smile, just-right handshake,
business card dangling at you like a worm on a hook. You
want to scream. You want to run. There is no escape; you've
been cornered by . . . a salesman! Sounds scary, right? It
probably happens to you all the time. Sometimes they want
to sell you office supplies or software or services; sometimes
they want you to join a project or task force or *(shudder)* the
volleyball team. Horrors! Salesmen and saleswomen cover
workplaces like weasels on a mink farm. Do the one thing
you can do: Protect yourself! Especially when hitting a *(gasp)*
trade show or meeting, keep this charm with you. You may
still get cornered, but the salesman will find you've slipped
away before he can say "ten percent discount!"

YOU WILL NEED
+ a hematite stone (easy to find in any mineral shop)
+ a few fresh sage leaves

THE SPELL
On a Tuesday at midnight, hold the hematite tightly in both hands. Touch it to your forehead, heart, and lower belly. Visualize power entering it and at each point, say:

PROTECT MY MIND
PROTECT MY HEART
PROTECT MY BODY
KEEP EVIL APART!
AVE MARS!

Rub the stone with the sage leaves, saying:

DEFLECT, DEFLECT
AWAY FROM ME
SELLERS AND TINKERS

LET ME GO FREE
BY LIGHT OF STONE
SO MAY IT BE!

Hold the stone close to your chest and visualize it
forming a bubble that keeps all irritating sellers away
from you. Keep it in your pocket, and when anyone
starts to give you a sell, rub the stone and will her
to leave—then watch her creep away!

The Really Stupid Customer Hex ("Can You Hold for a Minute While I Find a Pen?")

As if you did not have enough to do! They call you with dumb questions, they never have information ready, and basic concepts like *pay* and *buy* seem completely beyond them. You find yourself fervently hoping that this person has no offspring. You know what you *want* to say, *but* if you are not polite it becomes a business problem for you. It is sometimes more than one can bear. How do you handle morons without actually picking up a sharp object and . . . ? Restraint is necessary, but a little magic will also deflect the twits away from you before your blood pressure reaches dangerous levels. Let someone more compassionate than you handle them!

You Will Need
+ a purple pen
+ a red piece of stiff paper
+ a small all-natural cigar
+ matches

The Spell

Just after a new moon, on a Tuesday, gather the items together and draw on the paper an image that looks like this, ∫ saying:

ÌRE STULTUS
ÌDIOTS AWAY!
ÌRE STULTUS!
HEED WHAT Ì SAY!
ÌRE STULTUS!
BEGONE EVERY DAY!

On the back of the paper, with the purple pen, write the names of the specific people who you want to go away, or you can write a generalization (e.g., "All computer geeks needing advice").

Light the cigar and, holding the paper, symbol facing
you, blow a bit of smoke to the four directions and
then on the paper, saying:

WHAT YOU SAY MAKES NO SENSE
GIVE MY EARS AND YOUR MOUTH A REST
DON'T WHINE WITH YOUR PLEAS
GIVE ME REST AND SOME EASE.
IDIOTS STAY AWAY FROM ME
BY THIS SPECIAL SIGN
SO MAY IT BE!
IRE STULTUS!

Put out the cigar at your feet and scatter it around you.
Rub some of the ashes on the paper. Keep the paper with
you, under your phone, or even glued to your forehead—
wherever it will do the most good to deflect the fools! As an
added bonus, this symbol can be doodled on a notepad when
someone you want off the phone is blabbing at you!

Sexual Encounters
of the Office Kind

You want to have wild, uninhibited, grind-your-butt-into-the-desk animal s-e-x with somebody—got to have that coworker where it counts! Hey, wait a minute! That is lewd and anti-efficient and may affect productivity! Oh, what the heck, office romances and flings have been going on longer than offices have existed, so why buck tradition? This little spell is to help entice that special coworker into your arms. (Well, at least they will be magnetically drawn to you!)

Or (for a reversible spell) has that office fling already happened? Is it fizzling out? Want it discreetly forgotten? Use the end part of the spell and, voilà! No messy cleanup afterward! Hey, we are all sexual animals and you know what they say about all work and no play. . . .

You Will Need
+ a red candle
+ matches
+ a small vial of good sandalwood oil
+ a small magnet or lodestone
+ a little of your sweat

The Spell
On Friday at midnight, just before a full moon, light the candle. In the small vial of oil, place the magnet and the sweat. Concentrate on who you want to entice, then drop a bit of the mixture onto the candle near the flame. Say:

I call up the flame of love
Now fill (name) with fire
From below and above
(Name) is filled with desire!

"Cook" the vial over the flame and mix it up
seven times, saying:

FROM OUR HEAD TO OUR TOES
OUR DESIRE BLOOMS AND GROWS
YOU MUST, YOU MUST TURN
AND NOW SEE
BY POWER AND FIRE
SO MAY IT BE
I WILL TO LOVE
SO NOW LOVE ME
LASHTAL!

Put on the oil when you go to the office the next day, wear
something sexy, and that special person will notice you,
believe it. Then it's up to you to "cinch the deal"!

Need to "turn it off" or get rid of a lover no longer
needed? Make up this oil (or take what you have left
after the fling has flung), break the vial, and burn
the contents completely, saying:

FROM OUR FEET TO OUR EYES
OUR DESIRE WANES AND DIES!
YOU MUST TURN AWAY
AND NO LONGER SEE
BY POWER AND FIRE
SO MAY IT BE
I WILL NOT TO LOVE
SO STOP LOVING ME
LASHTAL!

Wear some of the ashes from the burned spell as a perfume
the next day. The special person will mourn a bit but will
gracefully accept that it's over. Then you can say, "We'll
always have the water cooler to remember. . . ."

Home Office Prosperity Spell

Home is where the heart is, but for some of us it is also where we make our bread and butter. No job security when you are self-employed, right? Striking out alone in the world can sometimes be a bit frightening. You just hope that your phone keeps ringing and that it is not only telemarketers who call. We salute those fearless entrepreneurs who are the brave freelancers of the world! It is helpful to have a little magic on the side to tilt the scales a bit. Have you ever wondered why some people are successful working out of their homes and others are not? Could it be that they have some sort of lucky juju that helps them out when business is in a pinch? This is a just such a handy little spell to increase business and to help you have more fun at it too!

YOU WILL NEED
+ some fresh pure wheat flour
+ fresh basil, rosemary, and geranium leaves
+ a small piece of malachite
+ a bowl
+ some water
+ a knife
+ a piece of string

THE SPELL
On a full moon, mix the flour, herbs,
and malachite in the bowl, saying:

BY THE MOON AND THE SUN
BY THREE SACRED HERBS OF EARTH
ALL WILL PROSPER THAT I'VE BEGUN
WEALTH AND JOY WILL NOW GIVE BIRTH!
HEIROS GAMOS!

Add water and slowly mix it all until it is a small ball
of fairly dry dough. As you mix, say:

> WHAT I MAKE
> NEVER BREAK
> PROSPERITY
> COME TO ME!

Form it into a ball and remove it from the bowl.
Press it flat so it forms a kind of disc. With the knife,
push this rune into the dough:

Carefully turn it over (use the knife if you need to) and
write the name of your home business on the other
side. Make a small hole in the top of the ball. Touch
the charm with both hands and say:

> FORTUNE, FREEDOM, AND HEALTH
> JOY AND GROWTH AND WEALTH

SO MAY IT BE
ALL COME TO ME!
RESIDE IN MY HOME
NEVER ROAM!
FIAT!

When the disc is dry and very hard, put a string through the hole and hang it up in the northern corner of the home office. Soon, in your future, a Fortune 500 ranking!

Easy-Does-It Software Installation Spell

Installing software in your computer, whether you do it or another poor fool has to do it, is always a bit touchy and sometimes is an electronic tornado of disaster. Remember the last operating system you installed that shut down everything but the microwave? Well, first read the manual (ha!) and then, just to make psychically sure, do this little spell before clicking the install icon. Conflicts will become a thing of the past!

You Will Need
+ a bit of sand
+ a stalk of dried lavender

THE SPELL

On the day of the dreaded installation, place the to-be-
installed CD-ROM or diskette in the computer. Take the
bit of sand tightly in your left hand and circle (or wave it
around) the computer counterclockwise one time, saying:

> SILICON TAKE
> EVERY FLAW AND GLITCH
> BIND IT AND BLAST IT
> AS TROUBLES I DITCH!

Toss it out a window, flush it away, or get it
out of there somehow and say:

> SVAHA!

Then, crush the lavender, gently releasing its perfume,
circle the hard drive three times clockwise,
and then touch it to the hard drive, saying:

İnstall without error
Begone all terror
Do us no harm
Work like a charm
Aum ha!

That baby should load like a charm, the system will not crash, your work can get done, and the world can continue to turn on its axis in relative peace!

THE TERMINATED TERMINATOR HEX
(THEY FIRED YOU, SO FIRE BACK!)

They canned you! Or they laid you off! Or they reorganized
your butt right out of a rent-paying job! *Grrrrrrr!* But you
know you'll bounce back better and stronger than before.
You know that the job sucked and they don't deserve you.
And you know that you want to get even, right? Well,
there is no need to "go postal" or get antisocial; channel
that energy into a slap at the morons who didn't
appreciate or deserve you . . . and smile!

YOU WILL NEED
+ a very small pocket mirror
+ some red pepper

THE SPELL

Before you leave the pest hole you have been ejected from, take the mirror and pepper to work. Turn around three times counterclockwise while flashing the mirror about. Aim it especially at the office or cubicle of the person or people who've really done you wrong, then whisper:

BACK TO YOU
BACK TO YOU
ALL THE FILTH
AND EVIL YOU DO!
WHAT IS UNFAIR
WILL BECOME TRUE!
KALIHUM!

Place the red pepper on the mirror, hold it with both hands, channel all your anger into it, and say:

MY ANGER FLOWS OUT
A SILENT RED SHOUT
ALL FEEL MY RAGE

In this battle I wage!
Kalihum!

Scatter the red pepper all over—especially
wherever the Bad Guys hang out.

Hide the mirror under the rug or somewhere it
will never be found. Break the mirror in its
hiding place (carefully!) and say:

I now go on
Anger here stay
They'll feel my wrath
A year and a day!
Kalihum!

Feel the Balance now—all the wrong will be put right,
instant karma adjustment! Now, go have a drink and
start the new exciting chapter of your life!

Return My Phone Calls Spell

You try and do your job; why, you sometimes wonder.
Why won't other people do theirs, right? We all know
voice mail is Pure Evil, and sometimes it seems that
there is no human under all those different computer
voices (press 3 if you want to kill the machine!). And to
make matters worse the yahoo you need to get hold of
won't return a *&%* call! Or maybe it is a fax or an E-mail . . .
and when he finally does respond, it is always with a lame
excuse, right? Well, no more. This spell will light a fire
under him, no doubt, and get a pronto response!

You Will Need
+ a red piece of paper
+ a red pen
+ some sesame oil
+ your telephone (or fax machine or computer)

THE SPELL

On a Wednesday at sunset, cut a diamond shape out of
the red paper and hold it up to the four directions
and then above you, saying each time:

DART OF WORDS
DART OF FIRE
BRING TO ME
WHAT I DESIRE
TELUS BURN!
MY CALL RETURN!

With the red pen, write in the middle of the diamond
the name(s) of the person or people you want to return
your call, then put some sesame oil on the name(s),
rub it seven times, and say:

HEAR ME NOW IN YOUR MIND
SELFISH ONE NOW BE KIND
DAY OR NIGHT YOU SHALL FIND
TO CALL ME SOON I NOW YOU BIND!
TELUS FUGIT!

Visualize that call coming through and then place the paper diamond under the phone, fax, or computer, after lightly rubbing the oil-mark on the machine. They'll be calling soon; then you can decide whether to screen their calls on *your* machine or actually talk to them!

Get the Boss off My Back Hex

So your boss has a problem. Why make it *your* problem?
I mean, the bottom critter on the totem pole always gets
a bit squashed, but there are times when your boss (or her
boss, or corporate headquarters, or . . .) just leans a bit
too heavily on your delicate and very precious head, right?
When pressure, stress, in-house seminars, new job duties,
restrictions, or whatever come piling on top of you too fast,
this little hex will tell the idiots above you to back off!
Won't that be nice?

You Will Need
+ three small nails
+ a small box with a lid
+ a portion of a rose stem with thorns or a
three-inch length of blackberry vine
+ some salt

THE SPELL

At the dark of the moon, at midnight, find a crossroads or a place where two paths meet. With one of the nails, draw a triangle pointing down on the sidewalk or in the dirt saying:

MOTHER KUU
HEAR ME TONIGHT
I CALL NOW YOU
TO MAKE THINGS RIGHT
Kuu! kuu! kuu!

Place the box in the triangle and place the nails in it, saying:

PROTECT ME WITH
THE NAILS OF VAU
FIGHT OFF OPPRESSION
HEAR ME NOW!

Add the rose stem, say:

WARD OFF EVIL
AND CRUELTY
OF ALL OPPRESSION
MAY I BE FREE!

Add the salt, and say:

EARTH ALL TENSION
AWAY FROM ME
OF OTHER'S CRAP
MAY I BE FREE!

Close the box up and hold it with both hands, repeat the first verse (Mother kuu, Hear me tonight . . .)

Then leave some salt for the dark moon and take the box home. Keep it in your desk at work or even use it as a paperweight! It will help keep all craziness at bay. Feel free to open the top and "let the vibe out" when you are needing a break from the BS!

Parking Space Spell

You claw your way through rush-hour traffic, still looking good, avoid the crazed drivers and suicidal bikers, and you are ready to get to work! And, whew!, on time, right? Ah, but there is just one little problem: where to park? Lots of people got there first, so it's time to swing into action and activate the Parking Spell!

You Will Need
+ a penny
+ a little beverage of some kind
(a dribble of any espresso drink is divine!)

The Spell
As you are filled with parking despair, look in the rearview mirror when stopped at a light or corner, rub the penny between your index finger, thumb, and pinkie of your left hand and say:

> I CALL THEE NOW
> ☉ GODDESS SQUAAT
> FIND FOR ME
> A PARKING SPOT!

Toss the penny out the window (don't hit anyone!) and say:

> FOR THIS BOON
> I OFFER THEE
> A SACRED PRAYER
> AND A BRIGHT PENNY

Then, while searching for a spot, mutter over and over:

> FILL ME WITH GRACE
> AND A PARKING PLACE!

Look for that magic spot—you'll find one soon!

When you do, offer a bit of beverage to the Goddess Squaat onto the curb and thank her when you get out! Score!

HEX TO STOP OFFICE BACKBITING

Nothing can ruin your day faster than interrupting a
nasty story in the rest room—and realizing it's about you!
How many times have we heard "He said that she said
that he said that *you*..." and realized that there was a
poison barb at the end of it—for you. The motives are
many: revenge, jealousy, pettiness, random spite, racism,
sexism... who knows why you are the target of gossip?
Don't turn the other cheek! Make it stop, with this:

YOU WILL NEED
 ✦ a business card or other paper item from your
tormentor or just a small piece of stiff paper
✦ a red marker
✦ some red thread
✦ a needle

The Spell

On Sunday evening, when the moon is waning, draw a pair
of lips on the paper with the red marker. If you know
who is spreading rumors about you, write their name
(or names) around the lips. Touch the lips and say:

Hush and shush
Your evil tongue
Be ye old
Or be ye young
Halt your gossip
Halt your spite
I conjure thee
Turn wrong to right!
Nihil est!

Then thread the needle and sew the lips shut with a simple up-and-down stitch. With each stitch, say:

SHUT YOUR MOUTH
STOP THE HATE
I STOP YOUR TONGUE
THIS IS YOUR FATE!

When finished, keep the charm in your desk. When you see the person in question, or just when you feel gossip is bubbling up again, take the charm out and quietly repeat the first part of the spell! The nasty one(s) will soon find other victims and you'll be left in peace. Or maybe they'll develop dental problems. . . .

About the Author

Sophia is an internationally renowned psychic and spiritual teacher with more than twenty-five years of experience. She was taught how to tap her psychic powers by her grandparents when she was a child. At the age of three she began her study of psychic reading, card reading, coffee-ground reading, astrology, and other forms of divination. She is also a professional photographer. Her Web site is at www.psychicsophia.com.